HOW I SURVIVED
FOUR NIGHTS ON THE ICE

PUBLISHED BY INHABIT MEDIA INC.
WWW.INHABITMEDIA.COM

INHABIT MEDIA INC. (IQALUIT) P.O. BOX 11125, IQALUIT, NUNAVUT, X0A 1H0
(TORONTO) 191 EGLINTON AVENUE EAST, SUITE 310, TORONTO, ONTARIO, M4P 1K1

EDITORS: NEIL CHRISTOPHER, KELLY WARD, AND MONICA ITTUSARDJUAT
ART DIRECTOR: DANNY CHRISTOPHER AND ASTRID ARIJANTO
DESIGNER: SAM TSE

WE ACKNOWLEDGE THE SUPPORT OF THE CANADA COUNCIL FOR THE ARTS FOR OUR PUBLISHING
PROGRAM.

THIS PROJECT WAS MADE POSSIBLE IN PART BY THE GOVERNMENT OF CANADA.
CE PROJET A ÉTÉ RENDU POSSIBLE EN PARTIE GRÂCE AU GOUVERNEMENT DU CANADA.

ISBN: 978-1-77227-272-7

PRINTED IN CANADA

LIBRARY AND ARCHIVES CANADA CATALOGUING IN PUBLICATION

TITLE: HOW I SURVIVED : FOUR NIGHTS ON THE ICE / BY SERAPIO ITTUARDJUAT ;
ILLUSTRATED BY MATTHEW K. HODDY.
OTHER TITLES: ANNAUMANASUARNIRILAUQTARA. ENGLISH
NAMES: ITTUSARDJUAT, SERAPIO, 1945- AUTHOR. | HODDY, MATTHEW K., 1984- ARTIST.
IDENTIFIERS: CANADIANA 20200203266 | ISBN 9781772272727 (HARDCOVER)
SUBJECTS: LCSH: ITTUSARDJUAT, SERAPIO, 1945---COMIC BOOKS, STRIPS, ETC. | LCSH: SURVIVAL--
ARCTIC REGIONS--COMIC BOOKS, STRIPS, ETC. | LCSH: TRADITIONAL ECOLOGICAL KNOWLEDGE--ARCTIC
REGIONS--COMIC BOOKS, STRIPS, ETC. | LCGFT: AUTOBIOGRAPHICAL COMICS. | LCGFT: NONFICTION
COMICS.
CLASSIFICATION: LCC GG06 .I8813 2020 I DDC J613.6/909113--DC23

HOW I SURVIVED
FOUR NIGHTS ON THE ICE

BY SERAPIO ITTUSARDJUAT

ILLUSTRATED BY MATTHEW K. HODDY

IT WAS DECEMBER OF 2008.

I TRAVELLED TO IQALUIT, THE FISHING CAMP NORTH OF IGLOOLIK, TO PICK UP SOME *MAKTAAQ* MY SON HAD LEFT BEHIND.

VROOOOOOM

I WAS MAKING MY WAY BACK ACROSS THE SEA ICE, GOING HOME TO IGLOOLIK.

THE OCEAN BETWEEN BAFFIN AND THE MELVILLE PENINSULA IS WIDE. THE ICE NEAR THE SHORE FREEZES FIRST AND IS COVERED IN SNOW, BUT IN THE MIDDLE, FAR FROM LAND, THE ICE FREEZES MUCH LATER. IT MOVES AND SHIFTS AS IT FREEZES AND BECOMES ROUGH, WITH VERY LITTLE SNOW.

. . . I ATE THE FOOD THAT I HAD BROUGHT WITH ME.

ON MY WAY TO IQALUIT, THE PULL CORD ON THE ENGINE HAD BROKEN. I HAD WOUND A ROPE AROUND IT TO MAKE IT GO.

I PULLED.

IT CAME ALIVE FOR A SECOND OR TWO AND THEN DIED.

>SPUT...<

>SPUT...<

STAYING DRY WAS THE MOST IMPORTANT THING ON MY MIND. GETTING WET CAN CAUSE HYPOTHERMIA, WHICH IS VERY DANGEROUS.

I REMEMBERED WHAT I HAD BEEN TAUGHT WHEN WE LIVED IN AN *IGLU*. I HAD BEEN TAUGHT TO PUT MY MITTS UNDER MY CARIBOU-SKIN BEDDING WHILE I SLEPT. WHEN WE DID THAT, WE WOULD WAKE TO DRY MITTS.

I PUT MY SEALSKIN MITTS INSIDE MY SNOW PANTS . . .

. . . AND SLEPT ON MY SNOWMOBILE.

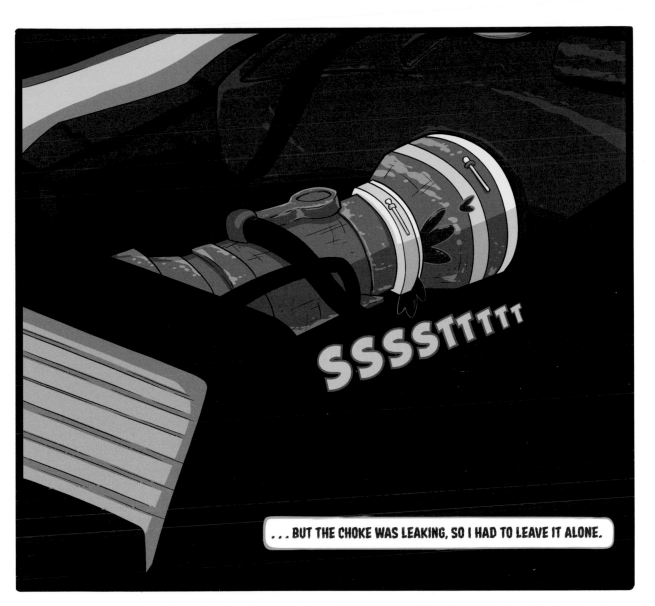

. . . BUT THE CHOKE WAS LEAKING, SO I HAD TO LEAVE IT ALONE.

I HAD WOKEN UP VERY THIRSTY, SO I TURNED MY ATTENTION TO THAT.

I TOOK MY FIVE-GALLON GAS CAN AND FOUND A SPOT THAT WOULD WORK FOR THIS PURPOSE.

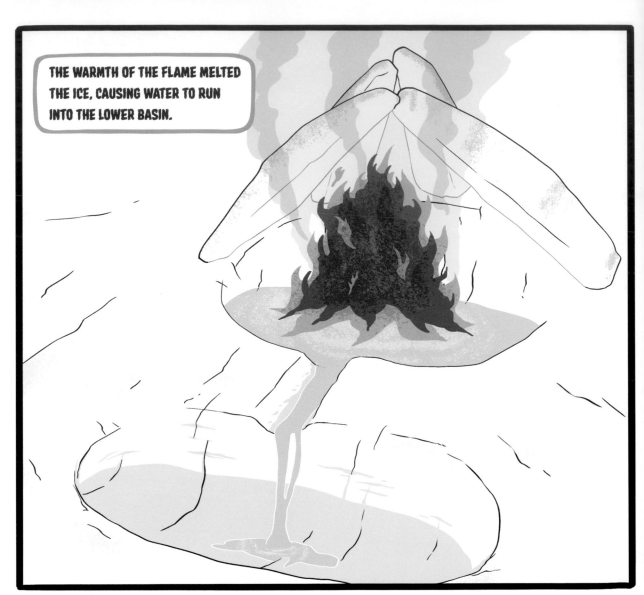

THE WARMTH OF THE FLAME MELTED THE ICE, CAUSING WATER TO RUN INTO THE LOWER BASIN.

WHEN THE ICE HAD MELTED, I TOOK MY HAND AND MOVED AWAY THE SOOT FROM THE WATER.

BECAUSE IT WAS DECEMBER, THERE WERE ONLY ABOUT THREE HOURS OF DAYLIGHT BEFORE DARKNESS FELL AGAIN.

I THOUGHT ABOUT CONTINUING ON TO IGLOOLIK ON FOOT, BUT I WAS RECOVERING FROM SURGERY AT THE TIME . . .

UGH

OOOHH

...AND WALKING WAS VERY PAINFUL.

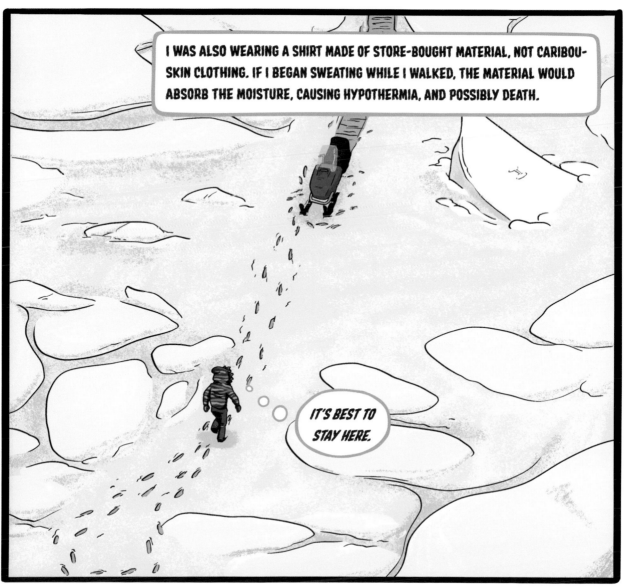

I WAS ALSO WEARING A SHIRT MADE OF STORE-BOUGHT MATERIAL, NOT CARIBOU-SKIN CLOTHING. IF I BEGAN SWEATING WHILE I WALKED, THE MATERIAL WOULD ABSORB THE MOISTURE, CAUSING HYPOTHERMIA, AND POSSIBLY DEATH.

IT'S BEST TO STAY HERE.

I KNEW A RESCUE PARTY WOULD BE SENT OUT, BECAUSE I HAD BEEN GONE FOR MUCH LONGER THAN I HAD PLANNED.

THE DAYS PASSED SLOWLY.

BUT THE PLANE NEVER SAW MY FLASHLIGHT
AND THEY WERE NOT ABLE TO SITUATE ME.

ON THE FOURTH DAY, I WOKE IN THE MORNING AND TRIED TO STAND ON THE ICE.

HUGGHH

AHH!

I FELL.

UGH

I TRIED AGAIN . . .

. . . AND FELL.

OOOF!

I COULD NOT STAND. I DID NOT UNDERSTAND WHY THIS WAS HAPPENING, BUT I TALKED TO MYSELF AND WILLED MYSELF TO WALK.

I WON'T GIVE UP, I WON'T GIVE UP!

I GOT TO MY FEET AND WALKED AROUND, TRYING TO KEEP WARM.

I KNEW I COULD NOT GET MY FEET WET, SO I HAD TO GET BACK ON MY SNOWMOBILE.

DARKNESS FELL.

EVENTUALLY I FELL ASLEEP.

VROOOOM

ON THE FOURTH NIGHT I WOKE TO SEE TWO SNOWMOBILES TRAVELLING CLOSE BY.

VROOOOM

I GRABBED MY FLASHLIGHT.

IT TURNS OUT A PARTY FROM IGLOOLIK TRAVELLED BY SNOWMOBILE TO THE FISHING CAMP TO LOOK FOR ME THERE.

THEY FOUND MY MEDICATION IN THE SHACK AND WERE ABLE TO TRACK MY SNOWMOBILE FROM THERE . . .

THAT IS HOW I SURVIVED. HOW I KNEW WHAT TO DO TO SURVIVE.

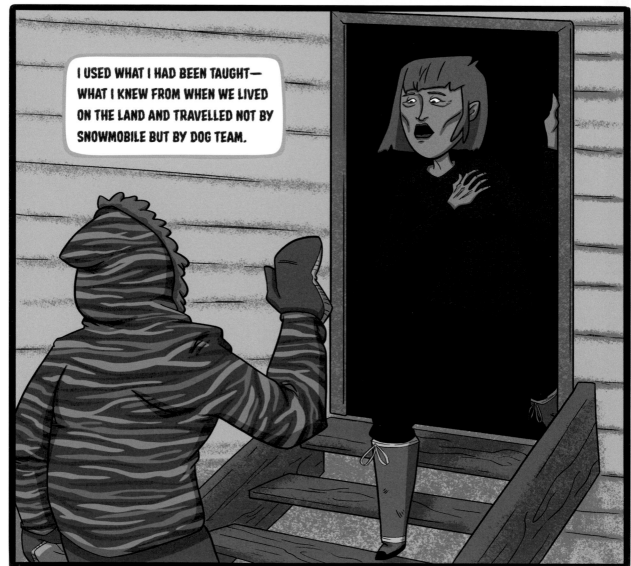

I USED WHAT I HAD BEEN TAUGHT— WHAT I KNEW FROM WHEN WE LIVED ON THE LAND AND TRAVELLED NOT BY SNOWMOBILE BUT BY DOG TEAM.

THOSE LESSONS ARE NOT JUST OF THE PAST . . .

. . . THEY CAN BE PRACTISED EVEN TODAY.

NOTES ON INUKTITUT PRONUNCIATION

THERE ARE SOME SOUNDS IN INUKTITUT THAT MAY BE UNFAMILIAR TO ENGLISH SPEAKERS. THE PRONUNCIATIONS BELOW CONVEY THOSE SOUNDS IN THE FOLLOWING WAYS:

- A DOUBLE VOWEL (E.G., AA, EE) LENGTHENS THE VOWEL SOUND.
- CAPITALIZED LETTERS DENOTE THE EMPHASIS.
- Q IS A "UVULAR" SOUND, A SOUND THAT COMES FROM THE VERY BACK OF THE THROAT. THIS IS DISTINCT FROM THE SOUND FOR K, WHICH IS THE SAME AS A TYPICAL ENGLISH "K" SOUND (KNOWN AS A "VELAR" SOUND).

MAKTAAQ	MAK-TAAQ	NARWHAL OR BELUGA SKIN
QAMUTIIK	QA-MU-TEEK	SLED
IGLU	IG-LOO	SNOW HOUSE
KAMIIK	KA-MEEK	A PAIR OF SKIN BOOTS

FOR MORE INUKTITUT LANGUAGE RESOURCES, PLEASE VISIT INHABITMEDIA.COM/INUITNIPINGIT.

CONTRIBUTORS

SERAPIO ITTUSARDJUAT WAS BORN IN A QARMAQ (SOD HOUSE) AT AKUNNIQ (BETWEEN SANIRAJAK AND IGLOOLIK, NUNAVUT) ON FEBRUARY 1, 1945. HE WENT TO RESIDENTIAL SCHOOL IN CHESTERFIELD INLET, NUNAVUT, AND FORT CHURCHILL, MANITOBA. HE HAS STUDIED ART, JEWELLERY MAKING, AND METALWORK AT OTTAWA SCHOOL OF ART AND NUNAVUT ARCTIC COLLEGE, AND IS A CERTIFIED JOURNEYMAN MECHANIC. SERAPIO COMES FROM A LONG LINE OF WALRUS HUNTERS. HE ORGANIZES WALRUS HUNTS FROM HIS SUMMER CAMP EVERY YEAR. HE ALSO GOES CARIBOU HUNTING WITH FAMILY AND FRIENDS. HE NOW LIVES IN TORONTO, ONTARIO, WITH HIS WIFE.

MATTHEW K. HODDY IS AN ILLUSTRATOR, COMIC BOOK AUTHOR, AND ANIMATOR HAILING FROM BRISBANE, AUSTRALIA. MATT CAME TO TORONTO IN 2014 ON A WORKING HOLIDAY AND NEVER LEFT. HIS WORK RANGES FROM MATERIAL FOR CHILDREN AND YOUNG ADULTS, THROUGH TO AUTOBIOGRAPHICAL AND INTROSPECTIVE WORKS. HE IS CO-CREATOR OF THE SPACE PYRATES AND SAGA OF METALBEARD COMICS.

TORONTO · IQALUIT